KULA

The Phoenix Who Rises from the Ashes

Cathryn Laverley Turay

TRILOGY CHRISTIAN PUBLISHERS

A Wholly Owned Subsidiary of Trinity Broadcasting Network

2442 Michelle Drive

Tustin, CA 92780

For information, address Trilogy Christian Publishing

Rights Department, 2442 Michelle Drive, Tustin, Ca 92780.

Trilogy Christian Publishing/ TBN and colophon are trademarks of Trinity Broadcasting Network.

For information about special discounts for bulk purchases, please contact Trilogy Christian Publishing.

Manufactured in the United States of America

10 9 8 7 6 5 4 3 2 1

Library of Congress Cataloging-in-Publication Data is available.

ISBN 978-1-64773-005-5

ISBN 978-1-64773-006-2 (ebook)

In memory of my late parents, Tom Laverley and Francess Laverley, for the love, support, and guidance they showered on me when they were alive; and the late KehTuray.

For my daughter, Frances Keturah.

ACKNOWLEDGMENTS

I would like to express my gratitude to my daughter, Frances Keturah Turay; my sisters, Francess Piagie Alghali, Juliet Laverley Amabebe, Patricia Nyanga Laverley, Rosaline Mamawa Laverley, Emily Laverley, Rev. Fr. Matthew Kanneh, Dr. Julius Sandy, and Professor Joe A. D. Allie, who all provided support and saw me through this book.

AN ODE TO THE BLACK WOMAN

The storm raged, and the billows rolled.
She stands tall, proud, strong, and serene.
The fires scorched.
She came out refined like pure gold.
She stands tall, proud, strong, and serene.
Everyone left her. She smiled.
She stands tall, proud, strong, and serene.
Her strength lies deep within. She feels bold.
She stands tall, proud, strong, and serene.
She delves into that strength and is cajoled.
She stands tall, proud, strong, and serene.
Knowing that she will never be left out in the cold,
She stands tall, proud, strong, and serene.

She is called Kula. She arched forward, reclined her back, and snuggled in the plush leather seat of the first-class cabin of the British Airways flight from Heathrow Airport London, which was getting ready to land at Sky Harbor International Airport in Phoenix, Arizona. She smoothed her long blue skirt and conservative tailored jacket made by her designer with African country cloth fabric. She was a tall, dark, exotic-looking beautiful woman in her mid-fifties who looked almost untouched by age and was taste and class personified. Time had not dimmed her glow. Her body was muscled due to constant exercise which left her age deceptively at thirty-five, and she wore very little makeup. She always wore her hair in braids, and the only jewelry that she was wearing was a pair of diamond stud earrings and a Rolex watch. She was straight of spine, moved with fluid grace, and carried herself like a Greek goddess. She finished her glass of champagne and plate of caviar and was looking forward to relax in her luxurious three-bedroom apartment in an exclusive gated community in Scottsdale with her two grandchildren. She had wanted an apartment large enough to accommodate her grandchildren.

The apartment building had all the modern amenities, a sauna, a jacuzzi, a fully equipped gymnasium, an Olympic-size swimming pool, a hairdressing salon, and a spa. Esperanza the Spanish maid who takes care of the apartment when she is away would have cleaned the apartment and kept everything pristine just as she liked it. She was also looking forward to go hiking the next morning at six in the morning to Tom's Thumb north side mountain in search of solitude. Tom's

Thumb north side mountain was easily visible from the Scottsdale area and provides some great views of Phoenix. It had a well-manicured lawn and was usually nice for hiking. She loved Phoenix as it reminded her of Bodinbo, the town where she was born, in Niinoa Limbo, West Africa.

In her mind's eye, she imagined that Bodinbo would look like Phoenix when developed and could not wait to feel the blast of hot air as she stepped out of the plane, on to the sidewalk of the airport unlike the cold weather in London. In Phoenix and Scottsdale, the weather was ideal in spring, fall, and winter. She loved the serenity and tranquility of the desert. The plane landed and taxied on the tarmac. Kula disembarked quickly with her two grandchildren as her aunt, Musu, and cousin, Fanta, would eagerly be waiting for them

She had worked hard, forged from her own hands, the product of toil and sweat, and had created and controlled a small empire in spite of the many setbacks and challenges that she had been through. Her success was rooted both in her strong faith in God, as well as solid personal achievements. She closed her eyes, and her mind went back, far back to how it all started so many years ago, and the sweet memory of childhood days came crowding back to her.

Childhood isn't just those years. It's also the opinions
you form about them afterwards.

—**Kim Stanley Robinson,** *Green Mars* (*Mars Trilogy*)

Kula woke up to the melodious voices of the nuns
singing "Ave Maria" during their morning devotion in the
Blessed Sacrament chapel at Saint Mary's Boarding School.
To her, it sounded like the angelic voices of heaven. Her
young spirit was immediately lifted up, and she could
feel herself being transported to a different world where
she mingled with angels and could even feel their wings

brushing her face. Heaven was very close to Kula. In her purity and holiness at age five, the veil that hid the supernatural world from the sensible world grew very thin. She could even smell the fragrance of roses in paradise. She remained in this euphoric state until the bell rang at five in the morning for her and the other girls to be up and ready to attend morning mass. She touched the beautifully cast sterling silver medallion of Saint Michael the Archangel that her grandmother had given her which she always wore hung on a thin silver chain underneath her nightgown and felt safe. The medallion was engraved with an angel with muscular wings who carried a sword and a shield. Saint Michael the Archangel is an emblem of strength and determination, of order and reason, overcoming good over evil. "Saint Michael will keep you safe," grandmother always told her. She braced herself for the ice-cold shower, particularly the heavy scrubbing she was to receive from Margaret the Senior Girl who was responsible to wash and dress her up each morning.

The day at Saint Mary's usually started with morning

Mass at six, followed by breakfast which was a simple fare of bread layered with a thin spread of margarine and a hot cup of cocoa mixed with a dash of powdered skimmed milk. Each of the boarders had morning chores to do before going to school. Kula's own chore was assisting to clear the cutlery for washing after breakfast. After school, the boarders had lunch (usually rice and either cassava leaves sauce or potato leaves sauce cooked with palm oil and smoked fish) and then went for an afternoon siesta for about an hour, after which they went for either needlework or Latin class. Next, there was recreation time during which the girls played a game of volleyball or tennis followed by the devotion of the month (Stations of the Cross during lent, the rosary during the Marian months of May and October and novenas) or evening Mass. Supper (consisting of bread and margarine and a hot cup of cocoa) was served at 7.00 p.m., followed by one hour of study, evening prayer, and bed at 9.00 p.m.

In as much as she missed her family, the formative years spent at St. Mary's Boarding School made a huge impact on Kula for the rest of her life. The strict discipline and regimented lifestyle she received from the nuns at that tender age prepared her to cope with the pressures and vicissitudes of life. Most importantly, it was at this young age that she felt the presence of God. She felt "the presence" (as she called it) most strongly at benediction during the exposition of the Blessed Sacrament when the divine praises were chanted particularly when the *Adoremus* was sung:

> *Adoremus in aeternum sanctissimum sacramentum*
> *Laudate Dominum omnes gentes: Laudate eum omnes populi*
> *Quoniam confirmata est super nos misericordia ejus*
> *Et veritas Domini manet in aeternum*
> *Gloria, Patri et Filio et Spiritui Sancto: Sicut erat in principio*
> *Et nunc et semper: Et in saecula saeculorum. Amen.*

Translated, it means:

> We will adore for eternity the most Holy Sacrament
>
> Praise the Lord, all ye nations; praise him all ye peoples
>
> Because his mercy is confirmed upon us
>
> And the truth of the Lord remains forever

> Glory to the Father, and to the Son, and to the
> Holy Ghost
>
> As it was in the beginning, is now, and ever shall
> be: World without end. Amen.

She would break out in goose pimples and remain seated for about five to ten minutes, enthralled! She imagined that this was what the spiritual writers refer to as "basking in the anointing of the Holy Spirit." It was at this young age that she developed love for the things of God, as well as a deep profound and mystic faith in God.

One afternoon, Kula was bullied and mercilessly beaten by Margaret (the senior girl responsible to take care of her) a short heavyset girl with thick lips and a brusque manner. She had stood her ground and refused to hand over her weekly pocket money that she had received from her parents to her. She prayed that her mother would come and whisk her away from boarding school. About two hours later, to her utter shock and consternation, Reverend Mother Anna came to their dormitory during their afternoon siesta and told her that her mother was here to see her! She burst into tears out of shock! Disbelief! Joy! Pure joy! She had experienced her first miracle! Even though her mother did not take her away from boarding school, yet Margaret, the short heavyset bully with thick lips, was expelled from Saint Mary's Boarding School. God had answered her prayers in his own way.

The Catholic Church's history in Niinoa Limbo may have started in the eighteenth century by Irish missionaries who were mainly Catholic priests. Saint Mary's Boarding School was opened by the congregation of the sisters of Saint Catherine of Sienna as an exclusive boarding school for young girls. The mother superior of the congregation was an Irish nun called Sister Perpetua who was invited by the Irish priests to take over the management of one of their clinics which was deteriorating badly. A cholera epidemic broke out during her stay, and she nursed the sick, gave instructions to many people who were dying, and even baptized some before they died.

At Saint Mary's Boarding School, the sisters accepted not only Catholics but also Christians from other denominations, as well as Muslims. There was no discrimination among the different Christian sects and the

Muslims. Kula's mother and her aunts also attended Saint Mary's; thus, her mother wanted her to follow her footsteps and possess all the sterling qualities that the nuns had instilled in her. These nuns lived long, fulfilled, and fruitful lives. Some of them who mentored Kula's mother (Reverend Mother Leo, Reverend Mother Anna, and Reverend Mother Patrick) also had the opportunity to mentor her. Reverend Mother Anna's warm smile could penetrate the very soul of a person. They not only taught the girls reading, writing, elocution classes, needlework, and home management but also Latin and music. They lived good holy lives and are responsible for the success of many great and successful women in Niinoa Limbo. Their modesty, nurturing, and love knew no bounds, and their faces beamed with a blessedness and peace.

Kula was from a strong middle-class Catholic family; her father, a civil servant, and her mother, a French teacher. They lived sheltered lives, were Lundu by tribe, and came from Nyandehungiebu village. Her father was born Patrick Kangiabengeh. He was a handsome tall man with a commanding presence, trim beard, a full head of hair speckled with gray and bold dark eyes. Irene, her mother, was a soft and gentle woman. She was the epitome of the proverbial wife in the Bible and possessed a quiet dignity and strength.

Nyandehungiebu is a small village five miles from Bodinbo. There is no road access for vehicular traffic, so the journey had to be on foot. When Kula and her brother and sisters went there on vacation in December, they had to walk the five miles on a sandy footpath. This was the season of the year that she loved most as it had stopped raining, and the sun rose every morning in its dazzling beauty. It was like a suspended glaring yellow globe that cast long black shadows over the footpath. The morning sky was an enormous stretch of startling azure blue that was an artist's dream to put on canvas. Birds soared overhead lazily, their wide wings catching the powerful currents of the wind. It was not too hot either as the coolness of the mountain night lingered and the cold, dry, and dusty Harmattan wind blew down from the Sahara Desert unlike the month of

March when the fury of the scorching sun blazed down on their heads. Some mornings, the Harmattan wind was quite severe, and a thick fog hung in the cold air.

Kula and her brother and sisters accompanied by an elder usually left quite early in the morning when the sun rose early, and the footpath suddenly began to throw up the heat that lay buried beneath it. The short shrubs and sparse undergrowth which surrounded the outskirts of Bodinbo gradually began to give way to fold upon fold of lush rolling hillside. They passed through several villages where some of the land was smothered in thick green forest. They sometimes came across an animal trail, and they made their way warily, thinking of hungry leopards. Once, Kula got something of a start when they reached the outskirts of one of the villages and stepped on a green snake. She took a hasty step back nearly losing her balance before she stopped. The snake wriggled for several seconds then turned and slithered away. Not until it seemed like there was no chance of it returning did Kula expel the breath that she had unknowingly been holding. *It was just a green snake*, she thought. Not exactly dangerous as it was not venomous and probably heading off to lie down somewhere out of the heat after the nasty surprise of seeing her appear.

It was a picturesque, delightful charming village with a river running through the middle of it. The fruit trees were laden with fruit, and birds chirped merrily in the trees. The water in the river was used for everything, from drinking to cooking, to bathing. It was a miracle that they did not contract cholera or any of the waterborne diseases. On arrival in the village, they leaped on Aunt Komeh, their uncle Sheku's first wife, like ants on sugar, plying her with questions and, in between the questions, telling her all about the family left back home and gave her the latest news about what was happening in Bodinbo. Their first port of call would be the river, where they would swim and play with the children in the village who looked forward to their visits as they would come with bread, biscuits, sweets, and toys which they shared among them. They swam in the river until they heard the *jemgbetutu* trilling *jemgbetututuuuu!* This indicated that dusk was about to fall, and they would then hurry back to their uncle's house made of mud and thatched roof to eat the sumptuous meal prepared by Aunt Komeh.

Aunt Komeh was the matriarch of the family in the village. She was a middle-aged woman, tall and strongly built, with authority in her bearing. She usually prepared cassava leaves sauce with deer meat, smoked catfish, and rice as she knew it was their favorite meal. It always amazed Kula that the rice was milled on the same day with a mortar and pestle that it was cooked, and the palm oil was also extracted from the palm fruit the same day. They ate the food with relish. She particularly enjoyed the smell of smoke on the food as firewood was used for cooking, sandwiched between three large stones set like a tripod. They loved the evenings particularly when there was a full moon as the villagers would all come out to sing and dance. The Lundu people of Niinoa Limbo are known for their love of music and dance. They sang ballads to their children to lull them to sleep and also sang and danced to give praises to men and women for their wonderful achievements. The young men brought out their accordions, drums, sticks, and the *kele*, and the women brought out their *shegurehs*. The drummers beat their drums with fervor and frenzy, in harmony and in sync with the rhythms of the *kele* and the *shegureh*, with the accordions weaving in and out of the melody. Men and women would clap their hands to the beat of the music reminiscing about the good old days of young adulthood with nostalgia.

On cold evenings after their bath and evening meal, they sat around a log fire with their shiny faces glistening with shea butter around their great grandmother, Soudie. She would tell them folklore in Lundu. The favorite stories were the ones about *kasilo* and *Nyandebo*. *Nyandebo* was an orphan who was very poor and had nobody to take care of her. She had gone through the rite of *sande* which was a period of education for young girls celebrating their transformation into adulthood akin to a prom and had no new clothes for her coming out of the *sande*. She went to the river every evening, crying to her dead mother who had been a *sowei* when she was alive. It was believed in Niinoa Limbo that when a *sowei* dies, the spirit of the dead *sowei* went back into the river as it was a river dwelling spirit. On the eve of her coming out, *Nyandebo* went to the river once again to cry to the spirit of her dead mother who lived in the river when she saw a beautiful *lappa*, silk brocade head wrap, a pair of beautiful slippers, and a pair of gold earrings, gold chain, and gold bracelets on the bank of the river. *Nyandebo* believed that it was the spirit of her dead mother who had left those things for her at the riverbank for her coming out of the *sande* ceremony the next day.

Great grandmother, Soudie, would personify some of the characters in her stories. For example, she would walk like a leper with her fingers and toes curled in shouting, *Heh mbe yorkor bennie yorkorah yorkor gbama.*

This was mere gibberish, and her great grandchildren would fall down on the floor, laughing their sides out. Sometimes they would just lie by her side on her bed, and she would tell them bloodcurdling stories of ghosts until they giggled with nervous fear.

Their lives flowed calm and smooth.

Then I said: "I shall die with my nest, and I shall multiply my days as the phoenix."

—Job 29:18, Jewish Publication Society Bible of 1917

Niinoa Limbo is a small country with an estimated population of one million inhabitants. The country was colonized by the British, and the first five years after post-independence was still impressionable. There were well-tarred roads right across the country, twenty-four-hour electricity, and pipe-borne water in most of the major towns and villages. Many intellectuals and professionals were

29

efficient and well-trained and the social delivery systems were well managed. The economy was buoyant. The British also left behind nicely built arabesque design residential homes (though not burdened by architectural frivolities) for civil servants with lush gardens. There were well-manicured lawns in front of the houses littered with flowers like hibiscus, bougainvillea, and roses. Fruit trees were often found at the back of the houses, and some of the senior staff houses had tennis courts. Kula and her brother and sisters became quite adept at climbing fruit trees. There were also large department stores with branches countrywide where Kula and her sisters obtained their weekly supply of their favorite comics like *Bunty* and *Beano*.

New cars were affordable and could be obtained through hire-purchase. Apart from the official car (which had to be parked at the Niinoa Limbo Road Transport Authority every evening and come back each morning to take Kula's father to work), her father also had two cars which be bought new through hire-purchase that he paid for from his salary. There was also a housing loan scheme through the government for civil servants. It was through this scheme that he was able to build a house.

One November, the legitimate government of Niinoa Limbo was overthrown through a military coup. The bulk of the support of this new group came from the northern part of the country. Unfortunately, Kula's father, Patrick, was not from that part of the country and was, therefore, victimized together with most of his other colleagues who were from the south, the Lundu tribe in particular. He was demoted from the rank of permanent secretary to the junior position of deputy secretary. Subsequently, a commission of enquiry was instituted to probe into the assets of former ministers and senior government officials. Fortunately for Patrick, its findings indicated that he was not guilty of misappropriation of public funds. Ethnicity and nepotism soon became the order of the day, and a very junior colleague of his from the east (who it is rumored) did not even finish secondary school) was appointed head of the civil service. He subsequently and unjustly sent Patrick on premature retirement. He was forty years old with a wife and four young children.

Irene, Kula's mother, had often warned her husband about taking a civil service job as she believed that it was time wasting. She often told him that the government squeezed you to your marrow. "Like orange, you are sucked dry and tossed aside for no practical reason," she often lamented. There was very little provision for civil servants in Niinoa Limbo when they retired. Most of them deteriorated very fast, both in their health and their finances. Despite these constraints, some civil servants like Patrick were honest with their jobs and maintained a modicum of integrity and dignity. It was usually regarded as a thankless job with very little reward. Patrick tried to get another job but to no avail. He tried everything everywhere but no way. The family could not survive on his wife's meager teacher's salary. They were especially anxious about their four children who had always been exemplary in their comportment and studies. How were they are going to take care of four children and solve a host of extended family and domestic problems? They would have to take a decision about Kula leaving Saint Mary's Boarding School and move out of the government quarters. They found a modest house in a quiet residential area in Nembe.

"The house can look just as good as our previous one once we have had the time to decorate it," their mother commented convincingly.

"All right, children, let us go now," their father commanded, gesturing to them to follow him to the veranda where their furniture and luggage had been packed. They followed him grudgingly then waited anxiously while he directed some boys to load their luggage and furniture in a lorry. They reached the end of the drive and gazed up at the house where they had lived since childhood with regret venturing into the unknown.

Irene was a survivor and possessed the natural instinct and reflex required for survival, daunting courage, and strength of character. Perhaps the steel in her character had always been there, unknown to her, for she did remarkable things for her family. Singlehandedly, she took up the responsibility and challenge of taking care of her husband, her home, and raising four children. She quit her teaching job and became a businesswoman. She traded in almost everything, from rice to fish and drinks. Thus she was able to maintain a decent home for her family, put food on the table, and pay her children's school fees. She maintained her small car, and when there was fuel shortage, she woke up at two in the morning to queue for petrol. She usually came back by five to prepare breakfast for her family and drive her children to school before she went to her small shop. She nurtured and mentored her three daughters who grew up to be outstanding women of character and stature. There is a saying in Niinoa Limbo that a tree was known by its fruit. Kula often wondered if her mother was the stronger person. "Could it be that women are stronger and more resilient than men?" She asked herself several times.

During the petrol crisis (a situation that often occurs in the country), this poor woman walked from her house to her shop, a distance of approximately four miles. She never complained and always had a hug for her husband and children. Because of her humility, her Catholic upbringing and faith in God, she never missed or reminisced about the good life she had before her husband's forceful, degrading and humiliating retirement from the civil service. For her, the glass was always half full. She would then count her blessings and look on the bright side of things. The burden that Irene was carrying soon manifested itself in her health five years after her husband's unfair, unlawful, and forceful retirement from the civil service. She became sick with cancer, held on for two years before she died, leaving behind a husband who blamed himself bitterly and four children who could not accept the death of such a lovely and compassionate woman. "Why then had God seen it fit to take her in the prime of her life and when they needed her most?" Kula asked herself many times. She was a young teenager of seventeen when she died. She felt a moment's grief, old and familiar as she thought of her unassuming kind mother. Her childhood had been filled with her tinkling laughter, and she could still recall the swishing of her *lappa* and the flapping of her flip flops back and forth as she gracefully glided from one room to the other to see that everything was in order.

As a young girl, she had been mesmerized by those swishing *lappas*, running behind her mother and would reach out to touch the soft fabric when she hurried off to another part of the house. In spite of her burden, Irene had been a happy woman and felt secure in the love of her husband and four children. Kula had to make a conscious effort not to think of the sweet, soothing, melodious voice that would never fill the house again or the smiling sparkling eyes that would never gaze proudly at them and the soft arms that would never hug them again "You do your father and me credit," she often said to them with warmth and hug them close to her. Kula glowed under her praise, hoping that someday she would feel and look just as self-assured and confident as she did. She also tried not to think of those days when her mother was alive and their home was constantly filled with relatives, visitors, and neighbors particularly during the holidays. Life was beautiful then. She wrapped her arms around herself, rocking back and forth. "The house will never be the same again," her father said with a sad shake of his speckled grayhead. "Not since the death of your mother."

Kula watched the sad look on his face wished that there was some way she could comfort him. He would sit on his favorite armchair for hours on end, staring into space, looking dazed. Sometimes he would sit up from the chair and look around in a confused manner, or bolt from it and simply walk away. It was difficult seeing the look of intense pain on his face, and she knew that he could not live without her as he did not have the strength and tenacity to cope with the pressures and vicissitudes of life. Kula secretly hoped that he would suddenly possess the characteristics of an eagle as eagles thrive best in storms. They use the very storms to soar to greater heights, knowing that peace is to be found above it. Isaiah 40:31 also states that,

"They that wait upon the Lord shall renew their strength; they shall mount up with wing as eagles; they shall run, and not be weary; and they shall walk, and not faint."

Unfortunately, however, he died exactly nine months

later, and Kula became the head of the family. She was eighteen years old and had just completed her secondary school education and was ready to enter university. She had passed the national school leaving exams with flying colors. She wondered how she was going to cope with no money and very little family support. She decided to put her university education on hold and continue her mother's business as she had to take care of her three siblings and support them at least to complete their secondary school education. She had learnt a great deal about the business from her late mother and quite capable of taking up the responsibility if necessary. She ran the shop herself, ordering stock, doing the accounts, and taking care of everything else that needed doing.

She discovered that she had a way with people, possessed the gift of the gab, as well as an acute business acumen. She needed a new challenge to take her mind off the traumatic experience of losing both parents within a year. She decided to embark on buying and selling *plassas* that came from the provinces wholesale to market women retailers, restaurants, and hotels. She sold the goods in her mother's shop, gave up the premises, and decided to rent a warehouse in the lorry park. Fortunately for her, one woman had defaulted in paying rent for her warehouse at a prime location in the lorry park and was forced to give it up. She established and entrenched herself in the *plassas* trade by developing her own effective marketing strategy, and soon realized that to stay competitive, she must keep unit costs low. In as much as the *plassas* trade was profitable, it was also risky as it is a highly perishable commodity with no preservation options available. There were produce examiners in the lorry park to grade and determine the quality of the various fresh produce as to whether it was fit for consumption by consumers. There was also a bevy of laborers to tote and store goods in the various warehouses. Lorry drivers and *omolanke* pushers carried the *plassas* in and out of the warehouses turning the lorry park into a bedlam of cacophonous noises.

She was lucky as the warehouse was large enough to provide storage for about two hundred baskets of *plassas*. She decided to avoid middlemen and brokers and buy directly from farmers to maximize her profits. Even though she had every confidence in herself as a businesswoman, yet she was not counting on those farmers to trust a young girl of eighteen right away to store and sell their produce. She thought of her aunt, Komeh, in Nyandehungiebu and knew that this was where she might prove useful as she was the ruler of womenfolk in Nyandehungiebu and wielded influence over women farm owners. All it would take was for her to recommend Kula as an astute businesswoman and a woman of integrity to deal with, and the rest would come rolling like a rock down a mountain. With Bodinbo's commercial networks stretching as far as the town of Karina, the rewards would be immense.

Kula also decided to stock goods that the farmers needed most up the provinces in her warehouse. She stocked sacks of onions and salt, bags of sugar, bales of cotton fabric, cartons of candles, and cases of rum. Her warehouse became a one-stop shop for the farmers who would sometimes take these goods in lieu of money as payment for their produce. Transporting *plassas* from the provinces to Bodinbo was also a lucrative business which she wanted to embark on as it was a direct link to the farm owners. She was also considering exporting fresh *plassas* to Europe and Asia, and she smiled broadly to herself accepting the challenge.

At the center of the lorry park was a community development bank which gave small loans to traders sometimes without requiring collateral. It dominated the trade in that area. Traders in that area depended on credit facilities upon that bank, and she decided to win the bank over in order to have access to credit facilities. She stopped a *poda poda* and instructed the driver to take her to the bank at the center of the lorry park. She also hoped that by going to the bank, she could get a better idea of the trade she could expect. Halfway on her way to the bank, she heard the sound of wailing and loud screaming. She looked back. There was a haze of thick dense smoke over the lorry park where all the buildings had been gutted down by fire. She paid the *poda-poda* driver and hurriedly rushed to the scene to see if her warehouse was spared. On seeing the angry flames like hungry lions licking and devouring her warehouse with a savage intensity, she lay on the ground stunned and fainted away.

She came around but with the wind knocked out of her. She could not speak for about an hour. She remembered a saying that Reverend Mother Anna always told them at Saint Mary's Boarding School, "It is not the number of times you fall that matters, it is the ability to get up from the fall." She cried uncontrollably, her body wracking with sobs. She was a fighter, but this incident was enough to break the heart of a lion. She quickly wiped her tears and had recourse to prayer. She felt cocooned in "the presence," felt peace, and, like a phoenix, rose from the ashes to live another period.

There is always some madness in love. But there is also always some reason in madness.

—Friedrich Nietzche

Kula was financially constrained and contemplated going to Nyandehungiebu, their village, to ask Uncle Sheku and Aunt Komeh to give her a piece of land to grow fruit and vegetables at the next planting season. However, the thought of being separated from her siblings was unbearable as they depended on her for everything. She decided to look for work and found work as a housemaid with a Lebanese family, Mr. and Mrs. Jaward.

The gargantuan house of the Jaward's sprawled out and stood high on one of Bodinbo's steep hills, overlooking the sea. She reached for the door and banged the massive knocker which was shaped like the head of a lion. After a period of about five minutes, the door was opened by an obese man wearing a white double-breasted jacket, pants in a black-and-white houndstooth pattern, white chef's hat, and a white apron tied around his waist. His uniform depicted that he was obviously the cook.

"The servants' entrance is at the back of the house!" he said condescendingly.

His scorn made her bold, and she raised her head in a show of defiance. "I am here to see Mr. and Mrs. Jaward," she replied icily. He admitted her into the house grudgingly. It was obvious that the cook wanted to throw her out but was unsure as he did not know who she was. He possibly thought of her as a threat as she was young and sprightly unlike his obese grotesque-looking self. "Mr. and Mrs. Jaward are saying their morning prayers and will be out shortly, you shall wait until they are finished. Whom shall I say is here?" he asked.

"Kula, the new housemaid," she replied. Her instinct warned her to bolt from the house. Bracing herself, she touched the cool medallion of Saint Michael the Archangel that her grandmother had given her for protection and felt safe. Steps sounded behind her, she turned and saw two men and a woman coming from a room which turned out to be the sitting room. One of the men was middle-aged and bald while the other was young with small beady eyes, a hawkish nose, and thin lips. He was Mr. Jaward's son.

The woman was young, dainty, and looked like a Barbie doll. She was wearing loud, ostentatious jewelry. She stared at her. Fortunately, her expression was not hostile but benevolent and as curious as a cat's.

"Kula?" she asked.

"Yes, madam," she replied. Her mistress was admirable and fascinating though at times, she seemed scarcely human. Her penchant for detail even the angle of a particular flower in a vase took its toll on Kula, but she took her duties seriously. She scoured the pots and pans until they glowed and never complained about her life of drudgery. Mr. Jaward's son, on the other hand, wanted her. She could see the lust in his eyes when he watched her like an infatuated young puppy. One morning, he returned from their shop leaving his parents behind. She was cleaning one of the bathrooms when he walked toward her, determination in his every step. Kula dropped the scrubbing brush, straightened, and turned slowly to the man who had startled her.

"I want to bed you," he said without preamble. It had been a long tiring morning, and his words infuriated her. She appeared to be distracted as if she did not hear what he was saying and looked on the calluses on the pads of her fingers and her chaffed red hands due to hard work. Suddenly, with all the force she could muster, she pushed Mr. Jaward's son, who fell across the bathtub and ran out of the house. She never returned.

She went back home, lay on her bed, and stared dry-eyed at the ceiling, not allowing tears to fall. It was not her fate to be raped. She must be content with the creature comforts of her life. She thought of her late father who made them repeat over and over again. "I am content with what I have, little be it or much." She had a full belly, a certain respect in her small community, and blessed privacy in her small room. She even had a measure of freedom compared to other young women of her age. Her gaze moved over her sanctuary that she had arranged with painstaking care. There was no clutter, only a handful of furnishings that she loved. Her bed, a chair, and a table which served as a desk. In one corner, she had put pictures of her late mother and father, the Blessed Virgin Mary, an image of the Divine Mercy, and the Sacred Heart of Jesus surrounded by candles which she lit every Sunday, creating a small family shrine where she could honor her parents and pray for the happy repose of their souls. Underneath her bed was a small suitcase that contained her most prized possessions.

Kula was unaware that she had finally grown into a beautiful woman. She had been as thin as a rake and flat as a board about a year ago. She had suddenly blossomed into a woman, and young men had come sniffing around her, lust wetting their lips, all of them desiring her. She grew to look more and more like her mother each passing day, beautiful, gentle, self-assured Irene. She was not interested in any of them as the huge responsibility of taking care of her siblings was paramount in her life and was not willing to give that up for a handsome face and glib promises.

Once more, she found herself jobless and penniless, and her youngest sister, Petifu, got sick with malaria. There was no money for hospital or drugs as she had just paid their school fees and bought a bag of rice for their feeding. Petifu lay shivering on her bed and had a high fever. She began to vomit painfully. Several times, she had sleepwalked, calling out the name of their mother aloud and expressing the desire to go to her. Kula placed her hands on her chest and back rubbing them gently, gave her a piece of ginger to suck, and the vomiting eased. She knelt beside her and started praying for a miracle for her recovery as there was no money. Instinct told her to wrap a hot-water bottle around a blanket and cover her body with it.

During some of their visits to Nyandehungiebu, she accompanied Aunt Komeh to the bush to collect the bark of a tree known as *gbamgba* that was used in making the medicine for the treatment of malaria. She remembered that the tree was found at the back of one of their neighbor's house, and she went with a cutlass to ask her neighbor if she could have some. She agreed, and Kula cut some which she boiled and gave to Petifu to drink. She also draped a thick blanket over her and the steaming pot of *gbamgba*. Her body was racked by a bout of coughing, and she sweated profusely. Petifu must not die. Kula's eyes became misty and tear-laden, and her spirit sank to a depth of depression. As the youngest, she always gave Petifu her special time and attention and would do anything to please her. "Please get well, Petifu, I will buy you a new doll," she cajoled. The fever broke and strength began to seep into her small frail body. She started to play, and Kula watched her with tears of joy streaming down her face.

She doubled her efforts to look for another job and got one as a sales assistant in a large supermarket owned by Mr. Bhagwani, an Indian trader. Kula had a way with people and the gift of the gab. Customers flocked into Mr. Bhagwani's supermarket, whose business grew tremendously. It was there that she met Abbass. He was of medium height with chiseled features, a strong jawline, kind eyes that smiled, and dimpled cheeks. He was a quiet and unassuming man and one of their best customers.

One evening, she was on her way home from work. Her head was covered in a scarf tied at the nape, and her gown was simple, drab, and unfashionable. Over her arm was the woven raffia basket she used to go to the market but not even her drab clothing or her market basket over her arm could make Kula look common. There was regal grace in the way she carried herself. She heard the soft purr of a car engine behind her. She glanced over her shoulder and saw a shiny black Toyota Prado SUV hugging the pavement. She walked a little faster, her heart skipping a beat a little quicker than usual, but the SUV overtook her and stopped. She came closer, and the rear window of the SUV purred down.

"Kula." She heard a voice call her. She stopped and looked into the SUV suspiciously. Leaning toward the window, who did she see but Abbass.

"I would like to speak with you. Would you like to step into the car?" he asked her.

She exhaled! Abbass Sanusi, the director general of the National Roads Authority of Niinoa Limbo! She did not know whether to be anxious or relieved. In front of her was one of Bodinbo's most eligible bachelors, a fixture in the local newspapers. She opened the car door and stepped inside, sinking into the plush leather seat as Abbass leaned forward to direct the driver to head for her house. She was shocked that he knew where she lived.

"I did not think that I would find you walking home," he asked her with quiet amusement.

"Is there anything that I can help you with, Mr. Abbass?"

Abbass nodded with amusement in his eyes as he was a man who does not speak much.

"I have been noticing you for months, and I like you very much. You are a very serious young woman, and I also heard about the unfortunate incident at the Jaward's house, as well as the loss of your warehouse through the fire at the lorry park. I am aware of your capabilities and ambition. You have a reputation of making it on your own merits."

Kula made an effort not to betray her surprise. It was unsettling how much this man knew about her, but Bodinbo was a small and close-knit community. "Thanks for flattering me, Mr.Abbass, but do you have anything else to say?"

Abbass paused, scanned her face, and said to her, "You are an orphan with three siblings that you are taking care of. This burden is too heavy for you. I want to ease your burden and protect all of you."

Kula conceded the point again a little surprised by the depth of the man's knowledge of her.

Abbass took off the cloak of bachelorhood, and they got married in a civil wedding ceremony at the courthouse in Bodinbo. It was a quiet ceremony. Her siblings came to live with them. Abbass' mother and two children from a previous marriage also lived in the house. Abbass was from the Jalonko tribe and a devout practicing Muslim. He also came from a polygamous home. His father had three wives. Had she made the right decision in marrying a divorced man? From another tribe? And another religion? Had she gone mad because of love? There must be some reason in this madness as this was the first time that someone had offered to lift the burden from her young shoulders.

Since the death of her parents, she had toughened up surrounding herself with a hard-protective shell so that she would not be distracted by the huge responsibility that was on her young shoulders. Maybe it was about time that she got married because in Niinoa Limbo, the dignity and status of a woman is considered incomplete without a husband. Aunt Komeh was apprehensive as she wanted her to marry a man from their tribe who was not a divorcee, without kids as she felt that she had to start life with a man with no strings attached, thus, no baggage. She told her that divorced people were usually problematic. She also referred to men and women who had second marriages with two sets of husbands or wives or two sets of children as secondhand people.

"Why do you want to marry a secondhand man, Kula, and have to cope with an ex-wife and stepchildren? The choice of who to marry is one of the most important decisions in life as it will dictate the entire course of your life and will be the barometer for everything else you do," Aunt Komeh cautioned.

Kula did not listen as she was in love.

It was as though her entire life had suddenly clicked into place, as though she had found a new meaning in everything she did. She hadn't expected to feel this way. It was the feeling of contentment that was the most important thing. The person who loved her just as much when she wore her scarf tied at the nape and her drab unfashionable blouse and *lappa* as when she was dressed in the latest fashionable *lappa* and fine jewelry. Abbass was a generous and caring husband and in absolute control of his household. He was firm, at times, rigid, but he could be very pleasant too. Naturally, Kula stopped working at Mr. Bhagwani's shop, and her husband opened a provision shop for her. To her delight, Kula became pregnant a few months after her wedding, so she decided to be a housewife and a stay-at-home mom for two years. She gave birth to a healthy baby girl who weighed seven pounds and nine ounces and had a full mop of curly black hair. She was the pride and joy of her life. Both of them doted on her.

"We are calling her Mariama which is the name of the Blessed Virgin Mary in the Koran," her husband announced.

Kula learnt from her husband that Mariama was considered to be one of the most righteous and greatest women in Islam as she was a chaste and virtuous woman. He also told her that she is mentioned more in the Koran than in the entire New Testament and is the only woman mentioned by name in the entire Koran who gives *Surah* XIX its name. Mariama's childhood as seen through the Koran and Islamic tradition is an entire miracle as she is believed to have grown under divine protection and was nourished daily by angels. He also told her that she is believed to have had daily visions of God.

"It is a special name," Kula replied softly, "for a special girl."

Her husband could afford to support her, and she found a shop manager for her shop.

It was through her mother-in-law that Kula developed an enduring love affair with growing things particularly during her pregnancy. Her mother-in-law grew vegetables and would talk softly to her plants.

"Plants need affection," she had explained when she surprised her one day in the garden, speaking encouraging words to a wilting okra plant. During her leisure time particularly weekends, she would work beside her mother-in-law, an apron tied around her waist. Within three years, Kula's little garden blossomed and encompassed most of the main beds. Wherever she knelt with her small spade, flowers and vegetables seemed to burst into bloom around her.

"They know you love them," she told her daughter-in-law.

One of Kula's sisters married and moved out of

their house, and her younger sister and brother won scholarships to further their education in the United States of America. She had been married to Abbass for twenty years and enjoyed the oneness with her husband that she had never experienced with anyone else. She felt safe with him and protected and cherished in a way that she had never felt before since the death of her parents. What she liked best about her husband that had kept them together for so long was his ability and willingness to shrug off any disagreements between them and act as though nothing had even happened. He was her rock, the person she depended on, and she did not want that to change.

Some people think that it is holding on that makes one strong; sometimes it is letting go.

—Unknown

Kula had a recurring dream. In the dream, she and her husband, Abbass, constructed a three-story apartment building at Peima, one of the quiet suburbs in Bodinbo. They stood outside the building which had been occupied by squatters. She became furious and accused her husband of bringing squatters into a house that they had struggled to build. She had the dream five times. One Friday afternoon, when she was in her provision shop, she had a fever and had to return home. Abbass joined her a few hours later. Kula noticed that he was subdued and quiet and was perturbed at seeing her husband this way. Later that evening, to her shock and horror, Abbass told her that he was going to marry another wife.

He affirmed her and told her that she had been a good and supportive wife who had always supported him in all his endeavors and compensated him with preparation of sumptuous meals. Be that as it may, he had to do a lot of traveling up country for long periods and needed companionship. He had just come from Hajj, was an Alhaji and did not wish to commit adultery. She burst into a fit of laughter like a hyena as she took it that he was joking. It was impossible! They had contracted a monogamous marriage. Law was made to regulate society so that people could not do as they pleased. Furthermore, she was a Christian. In the landmark case of the Niinoa Limboan Court *Kpukumu v Kpukumu* (1945) LR3 S and T 254, Justice Moriba gave the legal definition of civil marriage as follows: "Civil marriage is the voluntary union of one man and one woman *sui juris* excluding all others and performed by the appropriate government official with no religious rite." So what in the world was her husband saying! Niinoa Limboan law prohibited bigamy in civil marriage which meant that a person who had already contracted a civil marriage in Niinoa Limbo or elsewhere was not permitted to enter into a new marriage while the other person was still alive. It was a criminal offence in Niinoa Limbo created by section 17 of the Civil Marriage Act 1949. The law stipulated that if a man or woman whilst being married shall marry any other person during the life of the current husband or wife, whether the second marriage took place in Niinoa Limbo or elsewhere, that person was guilty of bigamy.

Could it be that her husband had gone mad? He could not possibly do such a thing because he obviously did not want to go to prison. The law in Niinoa Limbo is that anyone who committed a criminal offence would not be eligible to hold public office. He surely did not want that on his record. He grew up in a polygamous home and was familiar with some of the complications of polygamy. It was impossible to stay calm. She screamed! She fought! She jumped! She scratched! There was pandemonium in the home. Their daughter started crying, took a knife, and attempted to stab herself. Instead of her husband being contrite and remorseful, he became very arrogant and boastful. "He was a Muslim," he would say, "an Alhaji who had done the Hajj and an African."

Is this what being an African and a Muslim is all about? she wondered.

The quiet, gentle, unassuming Abbass had metamorphosed into a monster. It was as if his very soul had been possessed by an evil spirit. Kula almost cried out once again as Abbass' starkly masculine features dissolved into a mask of sheer ice.

"If I were you," he spat out from between clenched teeth, "I will try my utmost to stay away from me." He pushed her rudely, and she fell back upon the bed, shaken by the seething fury she saw in him. He went outside and slammed the door with a ferocity that surely shook the heavens and beyond. She was stunned to realize that she was trembling from head to toe. Pain like a tourniquet gripped her heart, and she curled up into a tight little ball like an armadillo. She shivered, envisioning anew the condemnation that blazed from his eyes sliced by it as if he was clearly there before her. She did not understand why he was so angry with her. It was none of her doing, she thought indignantly, yet he acted as if it was. Abbass did not return home that night nor the next. When he returned at midday three days later, his gaze pierced her as surely as a spear. Her hands were trembling, and she could barely unbutton the buttons of her nightdress.

"Do not look at me like that," she wanted to cry out! "I have done nothing to harm you. Nothing!" She looked at him with soulful eyes, warm tears brimming down her cheeks in mute appeal, but she encountered nothing but frigid condemnation and hate.

All of a sudden, her world turned dark and dreary, and the darkness fringed her vision. Dizzying incomprehension cascaded through Kula's mind, and she turned to stare at her husband, her face bloodless.

"No," she said faintly and then again, "No!" The cry that wrenched from deep within her was part despair, part horror, and pure anguish. Her knees felt like melting wax and almost gave way under her. She also became conscious of a faint buzzing in her ears. She suddenly felt herself swaying, and for a brief moment, she thought she was going to faint. She knew in her heart that the marriage was over because there was no way that she was going to practice polygamy considering her Catholic background and upbringing. There were going to be lonely days ahead, and she felt thoroughly abandoned like a stone at the bottom of a river. Once again, tears suddenly came streaming down her cheeks.

"Why?" she asked herself. Had they not been happy together? She sought permission from her husband to go for a retreat at Saint Kizito House situated at Lamanda Peak to seek divine guidance.

Saint Kizito House is nested on the top of Lamanda Peak and had been reconstructed as a small resort for the Catholic community in Bodinbo as a place of prayer and retreat. It was very serene and tranquil. Kula needed to go there to find the solitude and silence that her heart craved, as well as prayer and intimacy with God. She also needed to do penance through fasting as she had learnt that prayer in order to be fruitful must go hand in hand with things that are hard to endure. On the third day of her retreat, after breaking her fast, she took her Bible, held it in her hand, and prayed for divine direction. She then opened the Bible randomly to the book of Isaiah chapter 65. In her opinion, the chapter was about newness, from chaos to cosmos. She felt in her spirit that God was giving her a message in verse 17. The verse reads, "For behold, I create a new heaven and a new earth: And the former shall not be remembered or come to mind."

She knew that she had to move forward, to press on and reach out for the things that were before her and forget the past. The will to survive was there, putting determination into her bones and vigor into her nerves. God had given her willpower which most women of Bodinbo lacked. She decided to go and live in the house in Bodinbo that their deceased parents had built, which was vacant at the time. Out of courtesy and respect for her siblings, she informed them that she was going to live there, pay the correct market value as rent, and do the necessary repairs. To her utter shock and dismay, they told her in no uncertain terms that she could not go and live there whether she paid rent or not. Their callousness and insensitivity to her dilemma and predicament shook her to the very core of her being. It was as if she had a big wound in her heart, and raw salt had been rubbed into it. She did not have the energy to fight back or argue with them. Her brother and sisters whom she cherished so much and for whom she had sacrificed so much to the point of sacrificing even her own university education had not been sympathetic or supportive toward her when she needed them most. Her husband's betrayal was nothing compared to the ingratitude of her sisters and lack of reciprocity to the love and affection she had showered on them.

The following week, she received a letter from her landlord informing her that the rent for her business premises had increased. In fact, it had quadrupled. The letter also stated that the new rent was non-negotiable, and that if she did not pay the new rent, she was to move out and hand over the keys of the premises at the end of the lease's term which was the end of the month, a week away. The amount of money that her landlord was asking for was astronomical, and it dawned on her that her landlord wanted her out of the premises as there was no way that anyone could pay that amount of money as rent for that property. She had no option but to comply with the contents of the letter and made up her mind to move out. She later learnt that her shop manager had connived with her landlord to get her out of the premises as she wanted the premises to conduct business for herself. She also learnt that her landlord happened to be the boyfriend of her shop manager, and the rent that her shop manager was paying was even lower than what she was paying before. She felt dejected and alone, and her mind went to Psalm 118 verse 8 in the Holy Bible which states, "It is better to trust in the Lord than to put confidence in man."

In her opinion, she felt that it was no coincidence that this psalm is found in the middle of the Bible. Her husband and shop manager had betrayed her, and her siblings had abandoned her. However, the words of Saint Paul in 2 Timothy 4:16 came into her mind, "At my first answer, no man stood with me, but all men forsook me; I pray God that it may not be laid to their charge."

She could now feel and understand how Joseph had felt when he was betrayed by his brothers but was comforted by the fact that Joseph went from a prison to a palace after suffering thirteen years of injustice. She had to be strong and present a brave face to her daughter who had just turned sixteen and had entered the University of Bodinbo. The words of Saint Paul dwelt deeply in every fiber of her being, and she forgave all those who had hurt and abandoned her. She delved deep within her and immediately felt engulfed within "the presence." She felt consoled and, like a phoenix, rose from the ashes to live another period.

And who is my neighbor?

—Luke 10:29 (New Testament)

From her small savings, Kula rented a three-bedroom apartment for her daughter and herself. Her daughter had refused to stay with her father, had matured overnight, and consoled her.

She was her savior. To look into her pretty face and see the love in her eyes was the assurance that she needed.

"I love you, Mommy," she told her every night. She

was alone once more without the support and protection of her husband and was a bit perturbed by the loss of her dignity and status in living alone. She had once more become the beginning and end of all issues in her life. She felt frustrated about being without her husband as her days dragged lazily by, shrouded in despair. She was overcome by loneliness which had pitched its tent in her house as her daughter had gone to stay at the university campus. She felt it, like the deep-black color of the night, dark, thick, and tangible with no flicker of light. Each night brought the black embrace of loneliness. She hid her loneliness behind a serene mask of beautiful composure, and no one guessed it was there as she always projected an air of confident poise. She often contemplated about the propriety of drinking herself senseless with alcohol to numb the pain. She never had made up her mind that this would not be a good time to start and decided to take one day at a time like the lazy crawling millipede, cautiously and gently, one step at a time.

She had always been a selfless woman and had worked

very hard for her siblings and her husband, putting her own goals and dreams on hold. She walked up and down her apartment, wondering what to do, and realized that she needed a challenge and a better use of her energy. What was the purpose of her life and what problem was she created to solve? She had to have a bigger goal than marriage and kids! What need was she born to meet? What were the issues that plagued her generation and community that she may hold the solution to? She suddenly realized that, that was the starting point of every life's journey. Purpose births passion; therefore, she must choose a path she enjoyed or a cause she believed in and be willing to invest in. Maybe this experience was meant to take her deeper into self-discovery to raise her to a higher level. Whatever she decided to do, like a tightrope walker, she had to stay focused, keep her eyes fixed on where she was going, never to look back or down, or there was a good chance that she would fall. She remembered Reverend Mother Anna telling them that often, when God supernaturally closed doors, he also supernaturally opened other doors because he usually had something better for us. What was important was to keep the right attitude. She remembered Mother Anna also telling them that often, the greatest direction usually came from the greatest rejection.

As a young girl, she had dreams to study law and was fascinated with watching *Oponjo of the Lemplemp*, a Niinoa Limboan television series that came on every Thursday on one of the television channels in the country. The television series was created and written by Omari Lahai, a Niinoa Limboan lawyer. In the series, Oponjo Bindi was a scruffy barrister in Bodinbo who defended a wide range of clients often the downtrodden and poor people who could not afford to pay for representation. "The lemplemp" in the series referred to the criminal court in Bodinbo. Maybe her love for law and social justice was part of her God-given destiny. She went deep within as she always did and asked her spirit if that was the right thing to do at this point in time in her life. The answer came back to her with a resounding yes, and she made up her mind. Her intention to study law was to assist young girls and women who were in conflict with the law that were less economically endowed. She would offer legal representation to them pro bono as and when necessary. She sent in an application to the University of Bodinbo to pursue an LLB (hons) degree program in law and gained admission. She was thrilled and undisturbed that she would be attending the same university with her daughter and her daughter's friends. As a matter of fact, her daughter became her cheerleader and encouraged her to do so. She auctioned the goods in her shop, paid her tuition fees, and kept the rest of the money in the bank. Even though she was excited, she was a bit apprehensive as she had left school for a long time. She invested a lot of money in books which she bought from Amazon and was able to gain access to online resources like Westlaw and LexisNexis. She buried her whole being into the study of law.

Kula enjoyed studying law. She was awfully struck by the similarity between the parable of the Good Samaritan in the Bible found in Saint Luke's gospel and Lord Atkin's "neighbor principle" in the tort of negligence. In fact, the tort of negligence is derived from the well-known parable of the Good Samaritan. In the story of the Good Samaritan, a certain lawyer asked Jesus, "And who is my neighbor?" Jesus tells the story of the traveler, ambushed and injured by robbers and deliberately overlooked by the so-called "good people" who pass by. Jesus thus defines all our expectations of who or what a neighbor should be. Our neighbor is not defined either by social class, income, religion, gender, or ethnicity, but a neighbor should be someone who acts with compassion toward another person. In Jesus's time, this idea was preposterous as a Samaritan was considered by the Jews as an outcast or an outsider. Even in present times, many people are still challenged by the question, "who is my neighbor?" Simply put, it is "the golden rule" or ethic of reciprocity which is to treat others as you would like to be treated. The point that Jesus is trying to teach us in the story of the Good Samaritan is that we should treat people with compassion, even under difficult circumstances. Thus, her husband should have been a Good Samaritan to her and treat her with compassion, difficult as it may have been for him.

The "neighbor principle" in the tort of negligence is a principle of English law derived from the Christian principle of loving thy neighbor and the parable of the Good Samaritan. This principle was developed by Lord Atkin in the seminal case of *Donoghue v Stevenson*[1] also known as the-snail-in-the-bottle case. The story goes that Mrs. Donoghue met a friend at a café in Paisley near Glasgow for a drink. Mrs. Donoghue ordered a ginger beer float which was paid for by her friend. After consuming most of the ginger beer, Mrs. Donoghue was horrified to discover the decomposing remains of a snail in her drink. She became ill, suffered from shock, and had to be treated for gastroenteritis. She brought an action against the café owner, and later the manufacturer of the ginger beer in tort as it was not worthwhile suing the café owner as it was not his fault. The case created legal history, and the ruling established the civil law tort of negligence. Lord Atkin (who led the majority) held that a general duty of

---

1. 1932. AC 562

care could be said to exist between two parties under the neighbor principle described in his key quote. This is what he said,[2]

> In English law, there must be, and is, some general consequence of relations giving rise to a duty of care of which the particular cases found in the books are but instances. The liability for negligence… is no doubt based upon a general public sentiment of moral wrongdoing for which the offender must pay. But acts or omissions which any moral code would censure cannot in a practical world be treated so as to give a right to every person injured by them to demand relief. In this way rules of law arise which limit the range of complainants and the extent of their remedy. The rule that you are to love your neighbor, becomes, in law, you must not injure your neighbor; and the lawyer's question who is my neighbor? Receives a restricted reply. You must take reasonable care to avoid acts or omissions which you can reasonably foresee would be likely to injure your neighbor. Who then, in law is my neighbor? The answer seems to be-persons who are so closely and directly affected by my act that I ought reasonably to have them in contemplation as being so affected when I am directing my mind to the acts or omissions which are called in question.

---

2. 1932. AC 562 at 580

Lord Atkin's general principle consisted of two elements, the first being the element of "reasonable foreseeability" in which a duty of care would be owed in cases that a party ought reasonably to foresee that his failure to take care may cause injury to another party. The second element was a degree of "proximity" between the parties not in the sense of physical proximity but in the sense of close and direct relations. In short, an individual must take reasonable care not to injure others who could foreseeably be affected by their action or inaction. Mrs. Donoghue had proved her averments that she had an action in law.

Kula also likened and adapted Lord Atkins's "neighbor principle" to her current predicament with her husband. Didn't her husband owe her a duty of care? Why did he not take care and reasonably foresee that the action he took would likely cause injury to her and their child? There was a degree of "proximity" between them as well. He also owed them a fiduciary duty even though a fiduciary duty is often applicable in monetary and business transactions. A fiduciary as defined by Millet J in the case of *Bristol and West v Mothew*[3] is someone who has undertaken to act for or on behalf of another in a particular matter in circumstances which give rise to a relationship of trust and confidence. Hadn't her husband undertaken to act for and on behalf of her, giving rise to a relationship of trust and confidence? She excelled in her studies and graduated with an upper second-class honors degree in law.

---

3. 1996. EWCA Civ 533, Ch 1

Once a woman has forgiven her man, she must not reheat his sins for breakfast.

—Marlene Dietrich

Visitors who came in the middle of the night were never good news. Kula woke up to a loud banging on the front door of her apartment. The neighborhood where she lived was safe, so thieves were unlikely to knock on her front door, but she still called out, "Who is there?"

"Lansana and Saidu," they replied.

Recognizing the familiar voices, she swung the door

open. Her heart sank when she saw Lansana and Saidu on her front steps (her husband's nephews) and knew instinctively that something bad must have happened to her husband. She had been separated from her husband for five years and had not obtained a divorce because of her faith as a Catholic which condemns divorce. Having them show up with anguish in their eyes in the middle of the night did not bode well. She gestured them inside.

"What is it? Has something happened to Abbass?" she asked.

"Yes," Lansana replied flatly. "He collapsed about one hour ago, and we do not know where to go and what to do as we have no money."

She closed her eyes for a minute despairing, quickly composed herself, got dressed, and went with them to her matrimonial home that she had left for five years. It was her Christian duty to take care of her husband when he was sick, and they were not divorced.

Kula entered the house and saw her husband lying unconsciously on the floor in the sitting room and hoped that the tears in her eyes did not show as she did not want to lose her reputation of maintaining a cool composure in whatever situation she found herself. Apparently she later learnt, the woman he left her for had abandoned him for another man with more money. Shivering, she knelt beside him and cautiously spread her right hand across his chest. To her surprise and relief, there was a faint, slow heartbeat. He suddenly started coughing violently with spots of blood in his sputum intermittently. His breathing was also labored. They took him to his bedroom, laid him gently on the bed, propped his head high under two pillows, and kept him warm by wrapping him up in multiple layers of blankets. He soon lost his deathly pallor. She went to the kitchen, cooked some pepper soup, and made a pot of hot lemongrass tea that she picked from the garden. She felt disheartened that the garden she tended so well when she lived in that house had gone to rack and ruin. She slid an arm under his shoulder to raise him high enough to drink from the bowl of pepper soup that she held with a spoon to his lips. He was a proud man and found it humiliating that he was so weak that he could not even drink or eat without help. When he had had enough, she took the bowl away and gently laid him down again.

Panic surged through Abbas, and he was terrified that it was Kula who was looking after him suddenly remembering the cold, insensitive, and heartless way he had treated her, humiliating her deeply. The horror of that echoed and coursed through every fiber of his being, and he struggled to master his fear as he feared that she would avenge herself and kill him.

Seeing his fear, Kula took his hand between her palms, smiled warmly and assuredly, and said, "You are traumatized and have endured a considerable ordeal. Can you have forgotten that I am your wife? It is my Christian duty to take of you. Rest as I have sent for a doctor who will come and treat you."

Again he fought against rising fear. The emotion was a screaming, vulnerable, awareness that he was so helpless that it was the woman who he had mistreated that came to his assistance in his time of need and was relieved when the doctor entered the room and approached the bed. He examined him, gave him some drugs, and told her to take him to the hospital the following day for further tests.

Abbass was diagnosed with stage four lung cancer and had to be flown immediately to the United States of America for medical treatment as he had to go through chemotherapy. There was no hospital in Niinoa Limbo that had that facility. Unfortunately, he had no medical insurance, and each chemotherapy treatment including admission and other hospital charges cost approximately US $35,000 per treatment every fortnight. Both of them put all their savings together, and Kula took a loan from one of the commercial banks in Bodinbo to give them adequate resources for his treatment. They stayed with one of Kula's cousins in Denver Colorado, and she not only nursed her husband day and night but also stayed with him the entire time that he was hospitalized for the chemotherapy treatment.

Kula had been protective over her husband's business interests when they lived together. One of his friends,

Farouk, who purported to be his cousin as they were from the same hometown, had taken some goods from Kula's shop on credit and refused to pay as he claimed it was his cousin's shop. Kula persisted until he paid. On another occasion, he wanted to take a loan from one of the local banks and needed to put up some property as collateral. He pleaded with Abbass to put up one of his properties as collateral for him to give to the bank to enable him obtain the loan. Farouk married into a well-to-do family that owned a lot of properties, so Kula wondered why he did not ask his wife or his wife's family to put up one of their properties as collateral but instead had to pester and badger her poor husband. Farouk succeeded in convincing Abbass to give him the property to put up as collateral to the bank. He was reluctant to hand over the title deeds of the property after paying off the loan at the bank. Kula nagged her husband to ask Farouk to hand over the title deeds of his property which he eventually did. It was at this juncture that he developed a deep hatred for Kula. The final nail on the coffin was when once again, Farouk cajoled Abbass into putting up funds for a poultry business in their hometown. Abbass put up over 90 percent of the funds. However, as he was a public servant, he did not deem it fit to put his name as one of the shareholders on the memorandum and articles of association. As a result, Abbass put most of the shares in Farouk's name and the remaining shares in the names of his children.

When Abbass was undergoing his first chemotherapy treatment in the hospital, he told Kula to ask Farouk to give them an update of the business as they needed some money to cover some of the medical expenses. Farouk rudely cut off the phone and never answered her telephone calls again. Abbass begged his wife for forgiveness. Kula gave him her usual sweet, warm smile and assured him that she had forgiven him a long time ago, and that it was her Christian duty to take care of him in sickness and in health, for better or worse.

He could not tolerate the harsh and brutal chemotherapy treatment and died three months later. He breathed his last, his hand clasped in hers. She then informed his family (uncles, brothers, and children) that he had died. In spite of all that had transpired between them, Abbass was still a devout practicing Muslim and had expressed the desire to Kula that were he to die in the United States of America, he was to be buried immediately as is the Muslim custom. He also expressed that he did not want his body embalmed, let alone put in a coffin. His family completely sidelined her and did not even respect Abbass' last dying wish. They had his body embalmed, put his remains in a coffin which they flown to Bodinbo. She did not say a word but went along with them and accompanied her late husband's remains to Bodinbo to be buried. On arrival at her matrimonial home, to her utter shock and dismay were two other women whom the purported cousin, Farouk, brought to the house "sitting on mats" (as is the tradition in Niinoa Limbo for women mourning their dead husbands) claiming to be wives of the late Abbass and were mourning his death. The house was jam-packed with the relatives of the two "so-called wives," as well as a host of the dead man's relatives. One of the "so-called wives" had a toddler, which she claimed was the late Abbass' child. She knew that Abbass' family and relations, Farouk in particular, did that out of contempt for her because she was different and considered an outcast among them, being a Christian and Lundu by tribe. She knew her rights as a lawyer. However, she did not utter a word but maintained her stoic poise and dignity throughout the whole charade.

The death of her husband shook her deeply. He had been an honorable and decent man with a lot of integrity. What he did to her was normal to him as that was part of his culture, tradition, and religion. This was what he knew and grew up in during his formative years as a child. That is the reason why the formative years of a child are so important. In spite of their differences and the fact that she had moved out of her matrimonial home, he had never shirked his responsibility toward their daughter and took care of her until his death. She felt a tinge of regret that she may have been hasty in her decision to move out of the house as her reason for leaving (her husband's so-called marriage with another woman) had not lasted. However, someone had told her that once a woman has walked out on a man, it was never prudent to return. As a Catholic, she had been taught that every human being had a spiritual bank account. We either store up spiritual equity or iniquity by the manner in which we live our lives. Spiritual equity meant storing up treasures in heaven by the good deeds we do when living on earth. On the other hand, iniquity may be willful sins like murder, selfishness, immorality, and wickedness. The late Abbass had stored up a lot of spiritual equity in his spiritual bank account as he was generally a generous, kind, and humble man. Even though he did not want to be buried in Bodinbo, he had a befitting funeral that was worthy of a head of state that was well attended. Kula hoped and prayed that he was at peace and with God in paradise. She made a vow to pray for the repose of his soul until her own death.

Farouk was asked by the head of the family of the late Abbass to give an update and account of the general state of the business that he had been doing with Abbass as was the custom in Niinoa Limbo after the demise of a person. He informed him that the business was not doing well, and that he had taken a personal loan to inject into the business. He unilaterally took over the business and never returned the shares or a penny to the children of Abbass or any member of his family. She felt fulfilled and at peace that she had done all that she could for her late husband and had performed her duty as a Christian wife even though it left her penniless and in debt. Like the proverbial phoenix, she rose from the ashes of her life with Abbass to live another period.

Justice consists of what is lawful and fair, with fairness involving equitable distributions, and the correction of what is inequitable.

—Aristotle

Kula applied for a job at the Justice and Peace Commission of the Archdiocese of Bodinbo as her primary aim for studying law was to help less privileged young women and children particularly those who needed legal aid. She was employed as the gender officer. Kula and her team, most of whom were paralegals, visited the correctional facilities in Bodinbo and offered pro bono services to women and children whom they deemed necessary by virtue of their despicable vulnerabilities. This included women and children who were kept behind bars and forgotten about because the prosecution team did not attend court and those who had nobody to bail them. She assisted the paralegals to train the inmates in anger management as most of the inmates were victims of some form of abuse and always angry. Even when they took supplies to them, they pelted them with stones, and one inmate even attempted to break the windshield of the vehicle they went with.

In Niinoa Limbo, there were four types of law applied namely statutory, customary, case law, and religious law which sometimes create confusion that undermine respect for women's rights. The statutory law contained many discriminatory provisions which include the minimum legal age for marriage as fifteen years for women and eighteen years for men. The limitation age for women may even sometimes be waived to be lower under certain circumstances. Another discriminatory statutory provision was adultery. If a woman committed adultery, it was considered as a ground for divorce if committed by the wife. This did not apply to the husband.

Part of her duties was to take the necessary steps to ensure women's access to justice through developing awareness, raising campaigns, and encouraging women to teach their children and wards, as well as other women in their different communities the messages of forgiveness, tolerance, and compassion. In the family and grassroots communities, the expectation of peaceful relationships between women and men is usually cultivated by female messages of peace and human rights. Social workers working at the commission were taught how to succeed in examining issues of social rights that deprived women of their family inheritance by male elders of their families and other traditional rulers. In the event that women lost their spouses through death, they did not even dare bring up the issue of inheritance as it was considered a taboo. No one had ever dared to acknowledge the existence of this grave injustice to these women in Niinoa Limbo.

The Justice and Peace Commission of the Archdiocese of Bodinbo established good programs in gender justice, economic justice, land reform, democracy, reconciliation and mediation, and peace building. Kula's office was also used as a focal point for women's groups to raise women's concerns in the archdiocese particularly those dealing with issues of justice relating to women in society. For example, gender-based violence and rape were very common in Niinoa Limbo, and the gender office offered a means to pursue gender justice by revealing gender-related patterns of abuse, enhance access to justice, and advocate for reform. In working directly with women at the Justice and Peace Commission, Kula established what she had suspected all along that it is the woman who makes peace in the family. Women as mothers, service providers, and teachers instill in their children and wards core values like the peaceful solution of problems and conflicts which are the main qualities of sustainable peace.

Through her work, Kula became even more aware of

the host of challenges that most women in her country had to overcome in order for them to tap into their full potential. Most mothers, whether educated or not, had to work hard to put food on the table for their family day and night, and they had to multitask that with managing household duties. They had difficulty in accessing adequate health care in obstetrics particularly in the rural areas. Malnutrition in children was also prevalent. About 60 percent of families in Niinoa Limbo have women as the head of the family which was due to either the husband's desertion or spending their income on palm wine. The money earned by these women who are heads of their families is, of course, spent on the family leaving them with no extra money. Thus, they own virtually nothing. The majority of women in Niinoa Limbo do not have houses or any form of property in their names, and the secondary status of women has been buried deep into their very being. The rate of illiteracy in women and girls remain high, as well as the dropout rate due partly to the prevalence of early marriage, teenage pregnancies, and poverty. To access justice is almost impossible due to lack of information on rights and laws that protect women. High procedural costs also discourage victims from seeking justice.

In most poor families, girls are seen as a good source of cheap and free labor to do the household chores and to hawk goods, usually fruit and vegetables which they carried on trays on their heads from street to street or from village to village. Girls were also sent to the capital to work as maids for rich families as Kula herself did once. There was also the issue of young girls having to deal with early and forced marriages particularly to men who were sometimes old enough to be their fathers or grandfathers. The poor lives of these young girls seemed to be manipulated by others for their own selfish desires and conveniences. Hundreds of women in Niinoa Limbo are victims of rape, trauma, or physical injuries. There were about three hundred pending rape cases in the courts, some of them five to seven years old, while a lot more of these rape cases are not even reported, let alone registered.

There was this particular young woman who

benefitted from one of the Archdiocesan Justice and Peace Commission's microcredit programs who was twenty-three years old. Her name was Mamei. She was forced out of school by her parents when she was in sixth grade to marry a man old enough to be her grandfather. They had four children. She had two other sisters who were also married. Their father died leaving behind a fifty-hectares palm kernel plantation that he owned. Their uncles forcefully took over the palm kernel plantation, shared it among themselves, depriving Mamei and her sisters. Mamei's husband was an alcoholic and a womanizer. He was very abusive and beat her on a regular basis. She moved out of the house with her children, earning her living by selling fruits and vegetables in the market with money she got from a microcredit scheme from the gender office at the Justice and Peace Commission. Mamei had practically nothing in terms of material wealth, but she was always happy with a sweet disposition and always willing to help others.

Kula asked her one day, "Mamei, you did not get anything from your late father's property, and your husband does not support you and your children, yet you are always happy and content. Can you please tell me the secret of your happiness?"

Mamei told Kula that she attended mass every morning and obtained a lot of inner strength, peace, and inspiration from the Eucharist.

The empowerment of women, gender equality, and the realization of women's rights are central in achieving sustainable development in most countries. However, women farmers in Niinoa Limbo are central in producing food for their families but must often do so under increasingly constrained conditions. Niinoa Limbo is one of the world's most celebrated sources of cacao beans used in the production of cocoa powder, chocolates, and cocoa butter. However, women cacao farmers were marginalized, had very limited access to land and tools, and were excluded from decision-making. Kula's office formed a cooperative of smallholder women cacao farmers in Niinoa Limbo to enable them produce high-quality cacao beans, have better prices for the cacao beans, obtain easier access to land, more credit facilities, and also train and help them acquire the requisite skills in the production, drying and harvesting of cacao beans. The impact of this venture will not only improve their lives and benefit their families but also have a ripple effect and cut across the various communities in the country.

Kula was disturbed that companies who bought the cacao beans were making extraordinary profits from chocolate products whereas most of the cacao farmers in Niinoa Limbo were poor, particularly the women. She was a trader at heart and decided to add value locally to the cacao beans by starting a cottage industry in one small room in her apartment. She bought a small grinder, mixer and sealer, paid higher prices for the cacao beans to the women farmers than the market value, and processed the cacao beans into organic cacao powder (fertilizers and pesticides were not used by the female farmers as they could not afford them). The organic cocoa powder had a higher nutritional value than the commercial instant cocoa mixes. The Incas (an American Indian people) considered cocoa as the drink of the gods, an association which gave rise to the scientific name of the cacao tree *Theobroma cacao* from the Greek words *theo* (God) and *broma* (drink).

The demand for the organic cocoa powder increased countrywide, and the one-bedroom apartment became too small. She resigned her job at the Justice and Peace Commission to focus on the scaling up and expansion of her business but still offered her services pro bono to the commission as and when needed. She had been happy in her job and felt fulfilled as she had not only accomplished her dream of assisting women and children who were in conflict with the law but was also assisting in continuing the mission of Christ in her society by promoting human dignity, justice, peace, and the integrity of women and children both in and outside the church. Her work was based on gospel values, the social teachings of the church, a preferential option for the weak and marginalized and the vulnerable, a fundamental commitment to social justice, and the eradication of poverty. She was paid well, and through her salary, she was able to pay off the loan that she had taken at the bank to help her late husband pay off his medical bills. She felt gratified though humbled that it was during her tenure at the commission through intense advocacy with other female lawyers and other women activist groups that the parliament in Niinoa Limbo passed two gender bills into law. They are the Right of Widows and Children Inheritance Act 2012 which made provision for widows to have an equitable share of their late husband's property. The act also made provision for children to have an equitable share in the inheritance of their late father's property. The second bill which was passed into law was the Marital Consent Age Act 2014, which was meant to eliminate forced marriage for young girls.

She soon realized that there was a promising opportunity to enter the chocolate market as there was no local production of chocolate in the entire country. The country had only imported chocolates which were expensive and unaffordable to most of the people in the country. She experimented by processing the cacao beans, mixing it with locally grown dried fruit, nuts, and herbs. She tried different recipes, offering samples to friends and collecting their feedback until she created the perfect chocolate. She knew that to scale up and expand her business into a successful one; she needed a strong business plan. She enrolled in a three-month class in one of the local colleges in Bodinbo where she learnt about sales projections, finance, marketing strategies, and production costs. She also became a registered member of the Chamber of Commerce for Agribusiness Development in Niinoa Limbo to access new markets and sources of funding.

Kula leased a piece of land and built a small production plant to meet official hygiene international standards and increase her level of production. She promoted her brand, "Kangia Chocolates," through advertising in the radio, television, and newspaper. Within a year, her brand, "Kangia Chocolates," was on the path to success and was sold everywhere in the local markets and small shops countrywide, as well as supermarkets in all the major towns in the country. Her sales quadrupled, and the increasing demand for "Kangia Chocolates," soon allowed her to employ a full-time competent staff, giving preference to women. The chamber also helped Kula to expand to new markets by introducing her to potential clients in Europe and Asia through industry trade fairs and participation in conferences, seminars, and workshops. She soon started exporting the organic cacao powder, organic instant chocolate drink, and the organic "Kangia Chocolates," to Europe and Asia.

Her manufacturing business boomed, and she invested in real estate. There was a dilapidated hotel building in one of the prime residential areas in Bodinbo being auctioned. Kula took a loan from the bank, bought it, and refurbished the building into one- and two-bedroom-serviced apartments which she rented out to expatriates who came to work in Bodinbo. There was always full occupancy; therefore, she was able to repay the loan in a short time. She also bought a piece of land in the heart of the business district and built an office complex comprising of eight offices. Two of the offices were serviced offices that were fully equipped and essentially rented as a pay-as-you-use space. She built an ecotourism resort in Bassama, in front of one of the pristine white sandy beaches in Bodinbo and a house for herself in Lamanda Peak, Bodinbo.

A coconut tree-lined driveway led to the main house, a white building with a red roof, large bay windows, and a grotto dedicated to the Blessed Virgin Mary. The grotto was built with granite marble stones and surrounded by a beautiful garden of colorful tropical flowers. Outside the windows and far below was a formidable view of the city of Bodindo and the Atlantic Ocean. The house was sparsely and tastefully furnished screaming serene before it said money. There were white marble floors with high ceilings, white couches, white rugs with ethnic colorful abstract paintings and fresh flowers picked from her lush garden in Swarovski crystal vases. She also purchased two apartments, one in Canary Wharf, London, England, and the other in Scottsdale, Arizona, in the United States of America.

Breakups aren't always meant for make ups, sometimes relationships end in order for you to wake up.

—Unknown

With all of her accomplishments, Aunt Komeh told Kula that there was something missing in her life. As an African woman, she needed the love and protection of a man to enhance her dignity and status for her life to be complete. She had been wary and apprehensive of men and had not dated anyone since she separated from her husband. Aunt Komeh had rightly predicted that her marriage would not stand the test of time and had warned her of the inherent consequences of marrying Abbass. She told her that the marriage was doomed to fail because she had married an outsider, someone who was not from the same tribe or religion as she was and a divorcee.

"You should have married a Christian man within the tribe, someone who is not divorced," she often lambasted her. She insisted that she should start dating one of her own, a Christian man from the Lundu tribe, and consequently marry him. *Had Aunt Komeh gone crazy to even contemplate a second marriage for her?* she wondered. Was a second marriage really necessary? At this age and at this period of her life? For which reason and to what purpose? To please who? She had achieved without the support of a man, had she not? Little did she know that Aunt Komeh had handpicked a man for her. She introduced Bernard to her, a distant cousin of hers who was also from the same village as her. He was a politician in his late fifties, a fervent practicing Christian, and an elder in his church.

Bernard was short, though a bit taller than her with

a well-toned powerful physique, with thick muscular arms and thighs. His expression was devoid of emotion, and Kula suddenly realized she had no idea of what was going on in his mind which worried her, not knowing what he was thinking. She stared into his eyes which were as gray and as cold as ice. Eyes are supposed to be the mirror of the soul and echo thoughts of the mind. Could this mean that he was a cold man? Even though most of his hair had turned gray, that did not even soften his features. His face seemed to be carved from granite with no feeling at all. His mouth seemed to be too thin and his chin too firm. He did not look like the type of man who joked, laughed, or smiled. She felt a shiver of apprehension and desperately tried not to flinch from the chilling look in his icy gray eyes and trembled from head to toe. He frightened her. He noticed her apprehension and smiled, although the smile did not reach his eyes.

He said to her, "You seem to be scared of me, Kula. You need not be as I am your brother and will never hurt or harm you. You will be safe and secure in this relationship."

Kula relaxed and cautioned herself that appearances meant nothing.

Kula knew that Aunt Komeh loved her as much as any real mother could love her daughter and wanted the best for her. The reminiscences of their visits to their village came back to Kula and images and memories drifted like mists, opening up the mirror of remembrances. She remembered when her cousin, Kpundeh, caught fresh *makondei* from the river, dripping with water and held it up laughing. Aunt Komeh would quickly gut the *makondei* and prepare palm oil soup with rice mixed with jute leaves. She remembered the savory aroma of the food and the sound of Aunt Komeh's tinkling laughter as they went to wash their hands and devour the food with relish. These were fond memories, and for the sake of Aunt Komeh, she decided to give Bernard a chance. He had never been married but had two grown children from a previous relationship. Would she be willing to play the role of a stepmother again and would his children accept her? Would her daughter accept him? He was an offspring from a monogamous marriage with four brothers and two sisters. His parents were still alive, though both of them were retired. His mother had been a schoolteacher and his father a policeman.

Kula traveled to the cacao-producing areas one a month to buy cacao beans for her factory and to find out how the women in the cooperative that she had formed while she was working at the Justice and Peace Commission were faring. Some of them had even built houses. Bernard offered to drive her on one of those trips. It was a five-hour journey, and they left late in the evening, around six. Three hours later, the vehicle broke down in the middle of nowhere with no village in sight, and it was pitch-dark. She became numb with fear and had a sudden urge to ease herself. She came out of the vehicle and hurried off to do so by a shrub that was nearby behind which she spotted a small stream where she went and knelt down to wash her hands and face. She felt something move behind her and became startled. Fear coursed through her veins like adrenaline and was relieved to find out that it was only Bernard. He informed her that they had to spend the night in the vehicle as he did not know where they were, and there was no village in sight. He reached out and pulled her to her feet. His hold was firm though gentle, and he held on to her until they arrived at the door of the vehicle. She went inside the vehicle and attempted to stretch out on the front seat. She could not seem to get settled and missed the comfort of her bed. Bernard watched her try to get comfortable, opened his traveling bag, took out a sheet which he draped over her, went over to the driver's seat, and lay down beside her.

Kula did not understand his intention and became embarrassed by such an intimate gesture. Years of painful lessons in controlling her real feelings had served her well, and she maintained a tranquil expression and cool composure. His closeness was an erotic pull to her senses, flooding her with feelings that she thought had been buried deep inside her. She shivered from head to toe, finding out that she was only human after all. Bernard felt her shiver and smiled. Kula was taken aback by his spontaneous smile and almost smiled back only for her to realize that the smile was bland and did not reach his eyes. She did not smile back. Bernard was aware of the feelings that he had aroused in her and was amused that she was trying to hide them. He knew that he frightened her and tried to reassure her by pulling her into his arms in a warm embrace and kissed her. It felt rather strange, but she felt safe and knew that he would not take advantage of her or harm her in this, her vulnerable state. His warmth engulfed her and was lulling her to sleep when suddenly the wind whistled and brought the sound of beautiful singing from far away. It was probably coming from a *sande gomei* from one of the surrounding villages.

The *sande* is a female secret society that has existed in Niinoa Limbo for hundreds of years. The purpose of the *sande* is to assist young women earn the rites of passage from childhood into adulthood and educate them in cooking, farming, housekeeping, singing, dancing, and how to be good and submissive wives and mothers. The beautiful singing also made her remember two folklores that her great grandmother, Soudie, had told them about the *nuningayas* and the *sowei jeibu*. The *nuningayas* were mythical creatures who were half fish and half woman. The top part of the body was that of woman and the bottom part that of a fish. They lured travelers with their beautiful singing, then killed, and ate them. They lived in the river during the day and came out at night to catch and eat their prey through their singing. Their voices were so enchanting and bewitching that travelers would be drawn to their singing after which they would kill and eat them. Kula became scared and hoped that the beautiful singing they were hearing may not be from the *nuningayas* but from a *sande gomei*. She snuggled close to Bernard and covered their heads with the sheet to prevent them from hearing the beautiful singing. The *sowei jeibu*,on the other hand, was believed to be quite harmless and would come out at midnight to bring out the *sowei wee* from the river. The *sowei wee* is usually worn by the *ndoli Jowei* with a black raffia skirt on the occasion of the young initiates coming out of the *sande* and other solemn ceremonies like funerals. The *sowei wee* is made of ebony wood and has delicate feminine features like a small pointed nose, thin lips, ringed neck with a prominent forehead and an elaborate hairdo.

Bernard gifted her with flowers, chocolates, expensive jewelry, and wined and dined her in the most posh restaurants of Bodinbo and never asked for anything in return."Just love me, that is all I need from you," he told her. He was constantly in touch with her, called her four or five times a day, forcing her to listen to his never-ending declarations of love. He later introduced her to his parents. His father loved her, and they bonded in a way that any prospective daughter-in-law could dream of. He took her out for dinner one evening to her favorite restaurant, an exquisite and exclusive oceanfront seafood restaurant. They sat by the window gazing out at the ocean. It was a candlelit dinner with a bowl of bougainvillea on the center of the table with soft music playing quietly in the background. He took her by surprise by asking her to marry him. She then asked him to give her time to think about it as she was still apprehensive about getting married for a second time."What is there to think about?" he asked.

He stood up looking angry and perplexed, hurriedly paid the bill, and walked out on her.

Bernard stopped calling. Kula had not heard from him in three months. After three weeks of silence, she called him to find out if anything was wrong. He was very aloof and gave her flimsy excuses. She had her pride and did not call him back. She had felt fear about this relationship from day one. Her instinct had warned her that he was a cold and insensitive man who had the tendency to be quite ruthless. Even his features expressed coldness and ruthlessness. It was rumored that he had impregnated a teenager. Bernard who had been so warm and caring! Tears suddenly welled up in her eyes, and she swallowed a lump in her throat. She got a phone call from one of Bernard's brothers six months after their breakup, informing her that their father had died. Kula was distraught and cried bitterly as Bernard's father had loved her like a daughter. Fortunately, Aunt Komeh and Uncle Sheku were visiting from the village as they had to go and perform the *ngoyei* to the bereaved family which had to be done by a male as tradition demanded. When they arrived at the house, they were greeted by a nineteen-year-old teenager carrying a baby in her arms. Kula knew instinctively that the baby was Bernard's as they had a striking resemblance. Aunt Komeh was a forthright woman and did not mince her words. She asked without preamble, "What a cute baby girl! Whose child is this?"

"Bernard's," the girl replied who was young enough to be Bernard's daughter. She paraded up and down the house, holding the baby like a trophy to the embarrassment of Bernard's entire family.

Kula had been betrayed by a man yet again. This time, by one of her own, her cousin, a Lundu man who was a Christian and an elder in his church. She now understood the reason for Bernard's aloofness and withdrawal from her. Bernard had adult children and was even a grandfather, why did he need another child at his age? He was in his late fifties. She turned around and looked at Aunt Komeh with accusing eyes. As usual, she maintained her stoic poise as they went through the *ngoyei* rite. When they returned home,

Aunt Komeh burst into tears, held Kula's hands saying over and over again, "I am so embarrassed, Kula, how could I have known? I only meant well."

Kula did not say a word nor did she shed a tear. Instead, her feelings toward Bernard hardened, and some of the words of Plato's *Gorgias* came to her mind, "To do injustice is more disgraceful than to suffer it."

She smiled. Bernard was the weaker person as he had not only embarrassed himself but his children and his entire family. She delved deep within her soul thinking of St. Paul's words in Philippians chapter 4 verse 8 which reads, "Whatever things are true, whatever things are honest, whatever things are just, whatever things are pure, whatever things are lovely, whatever things are of good report, if there be any virtue, and if there be any praise, think on these things."

The words consoled her, and she banished all thoughts of Bernard from her mind. Like a phoenix, she rose from the ashes of her relationship with Bernard to live another period. Experience had taught her that from the ashes, a new life is born.

Our heart is restless until it rests in you.

—Saint Augustine

Kula opened the Kangiabengeh Foundation in memory of her late parents, a philanthropic organization committed to the education of the girl-child, particularly orphaned children and children whose mothers were incarcerated. This was because mothers were usually the primary caregivers in Niinoa Limbo, and if perchance the mothers are incarcerated, their children face a host of challenges and difficulties such as financial hardship which leads to the children becoming school dropouts. The foundation provided support in the form of school fees, uniforms, books, dignity kits, and nutrition packs. The foundation has supported over one hundred girls gain access to education at both tertiary and secondary levels. Other beneficiaries are trained in skills development and business management, which aimed to promote entrepreneurship among the young women. The foundation also operated a ten-bedroom emergency shelter for women and children who were victims of domestic violence, rape, and young children of incarcerated mothers. Children with incarcerated parents are an invisible or hidden group who are unacknowledged and do not benefit from the systemic social mechanisms that are usually available to direct crime victims in Niinoa Limbo. They receive very little support.

The mission was to guide these vulnerable groups reach immediate safety and fundamentally change the trajectory of their lives by helping them gain the knowledge, skills, and resources to succeed in life. Residents were provided with an array of services which included legal advocacy, individual counseling, and healthcare. One of the residents, Jebbeh, who stayed at the shelter was raped by her stepfather when she was thirteen years old. When she told her mother, she beat her mercilessly and threw her out of the house, accusing her of attempting to destroy her marriage. She became homeless without food or money and sought refuge at the emergency shelter. She had the privilege of finishing high school and later graduated from the University of Bodinbo. At her graduation party, she said, "The Kangiabengeh Foundation has shown me and made me understand the love of Christ. It put a roof over my head, gave me a bed to sleep in and access to an education that I thought was a pipe dream. I also met a community of peers who suffered similar experiences and understood what I had been through. It gave me hope to live again, and I am looking forward to a bright and rewarding future."

Kula invested most of her time to oversee the efficient running of the foundation as she believed that education was the sustainable solution to poverty particularly for women. She also believed that the dividend for investing in education for women was often higher than for men. Her daughter had married with two children and was involved in the day-to-day running of the business.

The conference of Professional and Business Network of West Africa (PBNWA) was hosted on a rotational basis by the Chamber of Commerce of the host country on the fifteenth of June every year. It was usually sponsored by the Regional Chamber of Commerce for West Africa and was hosted in Bodinbo, Niinoa Limbo, that year. Women came from all over the sub-region to grace the event. Kula had to give the keynote address and was celebrated as woman of the year that year because not only had she built a successful business, but she had also given back to her community in many tangible ways. She was accompanied by her friend, David, a tall distinguished-looking man in his early sixties who had flown in from Abidjan for the event. He lived at Lamanda Peak, Bodinbo, was also Lundu and a devout practicing Christian. He was an architect and owned a thousand hectares cacao bean plantation in Pandemba, the largest cacao producing area in Niinoa Limbo. He was modest yet powerful in his own way, a kind and caring man who lived to please her and was very fond of her daughter, Mariama. He had never failed her, never let her down.He smiled with his eyes and kept her grounded and centered. It just felt right to be with him.

"Why are you holding back? The man is crazy about you," Aunt Komeh pointed out several times over.

"I need more time. I am scared," she replied. She shivered at the thought of being intimate with another man. Kula closed her keynote address with the following words:

> Most times, the standard by which the world celebrates success is by the amount of money you make and the material wealth you own like houses, cars, and expensive jewelry.You can have all of that and still feel restless and empty inside. Like Saint Augustine stated in one of his most well known writings, The Confessions: "Our heart is restless until it rests in you." These are powerful words, and in my opinion, the only way that your heart can find rest and peace is resting and leaning on Christ.

> This can be achieved by making an impact
> on the lives of people you meet. For me,
> that is real success for at the end of the
> day, God will not ask me about how many
> things I owned, but the impact I made on
> my generation for the better good.

Kula left for her annual vacation three days after the event. The flight from Bodinbo to London was uneventful, and the plane arrived in London at 6.00 a.m. She went to her apartment in Canary Wharf and slept the whole day as a result of jet lag. She ordered Chinese dinner, which was promptly delivered, and she reclined languorously on the large couch in the sitting room in front of the television, eating her sumptuous dinner, and watching her favorite soap opera. To her surprise and horror, the show was interrupted as there was breaking news that there had been a coup d'état in Niinoa Limbo by a group of military soldiers calling their movement the Interim Patriotic Movement (IPM). There was a brief flash of the leader of the movement stating that the constitution had been suspended, as well as all political activities, and they were going to be ruling by decree until the next elections were held. He also stated that all cabinet ministers, high-ranking civil servants, and head of parastatals were to surrender themselves to the nearest police station or risk being locked up in prison. The announcer also announced that the overthrown president and his wife had fled the country and gone to seek refuge in the neighboring country of Bandekoya.

There was pandemonium in the capital, Bodinbo, as soldiers went on the rampage, looting houses, burning them down, forcefully occupying houses they fancied, stealing cars, and raping women. Many people fled the country and drove across the border to seek refuge in Bandekoya. Kula called her daughter who was also about to flee to Bandekoya with her husband and two children. A week later, her daughter, son-in-law, and grandchildren traveled from Bandekoya to join her in London. Her daughter informed her that the tenants who lived in her apartment building had been forcefully evicted with only the clothes on their backs. The apartment building had been looted and razed to the ground, and the soldiers had taken full occupancy of the tourist resort.

Kula sat down distraught. She was down but not out and a fresh surge of determination engulfed her entire being. What was she to do? She had lived in Niinoa Limbo all her life, a country that she loved so well was now under the control of a group of lunatics. She did not want to be a refugee, but most sober-minded people were fleeing the country. She decided to take the next flight out to Bandekoya immediately to monitor events close back home from there and join forces with like-minded people to meet with the ousted constitutionally elected president and his cabinet to find ways and means to oust the illegal military regime out. She left for Bandekoya the following day.

Within a month, the IPM (Interim Patriotic Movement) had killed over three hundred people and forced more than one hundred thousand people to flee their homes for fear of their lives in search of safety. Most of fled to Bandekoya which resulted in a large humanitarian crisis in that country. They did not close their border. This was a manifestation of their good neighborliness and solidarity with the people of Niinoa Limbo. Housing the displaced people was a huge problem as most of them could not afford to pay rent for houses. With the support of UNHCR (United Nations High Commission for Refugees), most of the displaced people were placed in refugee camps. Even with support from UNHCR and WFP (World Food Program), there was still limited access to food, healthcare, and educational opportunities for children. It was a difficult choice for people to make, to either stay in the underfunded refugee camps or risk safety by returning back to their country.

Kula met the wife of the ousted legitimate president, Lady Josephine, two days after her arrival in Musaya, the capital city of Bandekoya. She advised Lady Josephine to form a pressure group of like-minded women to lobby the international community for assistance to remove the illegal regime from power. Lady Josephine formed the pressure group comprising of female politicians, lawyers, doctors, schoolteachers, market women, and representatives from civil society organizations. Lady Josephine was the chairperson of the group and Kula the vice chairperson. The aim of the pressure group was to establish personal contact with heads of states of the neighboring countries, the African Union Commission, the United Nations, and the Commonwealth of Nations to present the sorry state of affairs in the country. There was no security in the country; there were random killings of innocent civilians by the illegal regime, raping of women, and other atrocities. The group also decided to contact leading journalists in the world to conduct slick media campaigns for the return of the democratically elected government.

A delegation of the pressure group traveled to the United States of America to lobby the United Nations to take appropriate measures to force the illegal regime hand over power to the legitimate government. Kula was part of that delegation. The group succeeded because the security council adopted a resolution that all member states should prevent selling or supplying arms and ammunition to the illegal regime, and a travel ban was imposed on members of the illegal regime including their families. The group also lobbied the African Union Commission to condemn the coup which it did and also succeeded in getting the

Commonwealth of Nations to suspend Niinoa Limbo from the Commonwealth until the democratically elected government was reinstated to power.

Apart from being a lobbyist and an activist, Kula also provided humanitarian services to the refugees. She rented an apartment building of four floors. Two floors were used as a shelter for single mothers with young children, and one floor was used as a school. Teachers who were refugees taught in the school and received salaries from the pressure group. Another floor was used as a health center which was efficiently run by one of the members of the pressure group who was a medical doctor. She also assisted in providing food and other logistics needed to the refugees.

In spite of the condemnation of the coup by the whole world, the military regime refused to relinquish power. It became apparent that the illegal regime would only be removed by force. The heads of states of the neighboring countries agreed on military intervention and sent a joint force with loyal soldiers of the legitimate government who were able to flush out the illegal regime and overturn the coup.

Kula returned to her beloved Bodinbo exhilarated, though exhausted. She had to build her apartment building from scratch and renovate her tourist resort in Bassama which had been completely vandalized by the soldiers. Her daughter also came back from London with her husband and two children. Fortunately, her son-in-law was a civil engineer and had his own construction company.

"You don't have to worry, Mummy. I will help in rebuilding the apartment building, as well as renovating the tourist resort," he told her.

She smiled and was happy. God had blessed her with a son as a son-in-law. Her daughter had studied economics and followed her footsteps by becoming an astute business woman. She decided to take a long vacation in her luxury apartment in Scottsdale as the nine-month sojourn in Bandekoya had taken its toll on her. She had missed her grandchildren and decided to take them with her. Her daughter and son-in-law were quite capable of looking after the business in her absence.

She would leave her legacy to her two lovely

grandchildren, the Kangiabengeh Foundation in particular, as she wanted the foundation to pass on from one generation to the next to continue the mission of Christ in assisting the disadvantaged, the less privileged, and the vulnerable. The Kangiabengeh Foundation showed love, and when you show love, you show God to the world.

The Phoenix

She dies in a fiery furnace

Consumed by the angry, ferocious flames

Yet she rises time and time again

From the cold black ashes of her pyre

More glorious and more beautiful…

Her plumage shimmers brightly in a myriad of colors.

Her legs are covered in yellow-gold scales with rose-
colored talons.

Her eyes blaze like blue diamonds.

She flies upward above the clouds to the smiling sun.

Singing with her beautiful enchanting voice.

Confident and bold

Stronger and wiser

To live another period…

GLOSSARY

Ave Maria. Hail Mary.

Gbamgba. Bark of a tree used in the treatment of malaria.

Jemgbetutu. Small African bird.

Jemgbetututuuu. Trilling sound.

Kasilo. Spiderman.

Kele. Some type of African musical instrument with a tinkling sound.

Lappa. Long piece of cloth that is tied like a wraparound skirt.

Makondei. Catfish.

Ndoli Jowei. Dancing **Sowei.**

Ngoyei. Condolence rite.

Nuningayas. Mermaids.

Plassas. Some type of green leafy vegetable.

Poda.A type of van used to transport passengers.

Sande. Female secret society.

Sande gomei. Female secret society dance.

Shegureh. Small calabash like musical instrument set with colorful beads and cowries.

Sowei. Leader of the **sande.**

Sowei jeibu. Sowei who lives under the river.

Sowei wee. Head mask of the **Sowei.**

Surah. Name for a chapter of the Koran.

Cathryn Turay is a lawyer who lives and works in Sierra Leone. She is a graduate in law (LLB) with honors from Northumbria University, Newcastle, United Kingdom, and a graduate from the Sierra Leone Law School. She is a member of the board of directors CARITAS Freetown, Sierra Leone, a member of LAWYERS (Legal Access through Women Yearning for Equality Rights and Social Justice, Freetown, Sierra Leone) and a member of the Sierra Leone Bar Association. She is widowed with one daughter.

CPSIA information can be obtained
at www.ICGtesting.com
Printed in the USA
LVHW030449240520
656397LV00004B/469